BC

M·A·R·Y

Prayers in Honor of the Blessed Virgin Mary

Secretariat
Bishops' Committee on the Liturgy
National Conference of Catholic Bishops

In its planning document, as approved by the general member-
ship of the National Conference of Catholic Bishops in
November 1986, the Secretariat of the bishops' Committee on
the Liturgy was authorized to prepare devotional Marian
resources. The *Book of Mary: Prayers in Honor of the Blessed
Virgin Mary* was approved for publication by the members of
the bishops' Committee on the Liturgy on March 23, 1987, and
is authorized for publication by the undersigned.

Monsignor Daniel F. Hoye
General Secretary
NCCB/USCC

Excerpts from the English translation of *Lectionary for Mass* ©
1969, International Committee on English in the Liturgy, Inc.
(ICEL); excerpts from the English translation of *The Liturgy of
the Hours* © 1974, ICEL; excerpts from the English translation
of *A Book of Prayers* © 1982, ICEL; excerpts from the English
translation of *Documents on the Liturgy, 1963-1979: Conciliar,
Papal, and Curial Texts* © 1982, ICEL. All rights reserved.

Selections from "Akathist Hymn" and "Theotokus Hymn" are
taken from *Mother of God* © 1982 by Lawrence Cunningham,
Scala Books (HarperCollins) and are used with permission.

Cover illustration by Laurel Vaughan, based upon Muttergottes
von Korssum and used with permission of Aries Verlag Paul
Johannes Müller; Feldkirchen, West Germany.

ISBN 1-55586-155-5

First Printing, June 1987
Eighth Printing, January 2001

Contents

Foreword

In his apostolic exhortation *Marialis cultus*, Pope Paul VI stated that "even as she is the model of the Church as a whole in its worship of God, Mary is clearly also the *teacher of devotion* for individual Christians" (no. 21). For, the Blessed Virgin magnified and praised the Lord for the great things God accomplished in her, his lowly servant. As St. Ambrose says, "May the mind of Mary be in all to magnify the Lord; her spirit, to rejoice in God."

The Mother of God stands at the center of the Church's devotional life, both as the teacher and object of devotion. This was clearly reaffirmed by the Second Vatican Council in the "Dogmatic Constitution on the Church," *Lumen Gentium:* "Mary, as the Mother of God, placed by grace next to her Son above all angels and saints, has shared in the mysteries of Christ and is justly honored by a special veneration in the Church" (no. 66). The Council taught that devotion to the Mother of God

as it has always existed in the Church, even though it is altogether special, is essentially distinct from the worship of adoration paid equally to the Word incarnate, the Father, and the Holy Spirit. Honoring Mary contributes to that adoration. For the various forms of Marian devotion, sanctioned by the Church within the limits of sound orthodoxy and suited to circumstances of time and place as well as to the character and culture of peoples, have the effect that as we honor the

Mother, we also truly know the Son and give love, glory, and obedience to him, through whom all things have their being (see Col 1:15-16) and, "in whom it has pleased the eternal Father that all fullness should dwell" (Col 1:19) (ibid.).

The Second Vatican Council expressly professed the Church's teaching on Mary and counseled "all the Church's children to foster wholeheartedly the cultus —especially the liturgical cultus—of the Blessed Virgin" (ibid., no. 67). And, in response to that conciliar teaching, Pope Paul VI, in the apostolic exhortation *Marialis cultus* (February 2, 1974), specifically called for the renewal of devotions to the Virgin Mary:

. . . the faithful's devotion and acts of veneration toward the Mother of God have also taken different forms, corresponding to historical and local circumstances and varying attitudes and cultures of peoples. One result is that the forms expressing devotion and subject to the conditions of the times seem in need of a reform that will eliminate the ephemeral, retain what is of enduring value, and integrate those truths of faith that have been reached from theological investigation and affirmed by the Church's magisterium (no. 24).

This collection of Marian devotions is an attempt to respond to both the Council's teaching on Marian devotion and that of Pope Paul VI in *Marialis cultus*. In the context of that teaching, Pope John Paul II, on the solemnity of Mary, Mother of God (January 1, 1987), proclaimed a Marian Year to commence on Pentecost, June 7, 1987, and to conclude on the solemnity of the Assumption, August 15, 1988. The purpose of the Marian Year is stated by Pope John Paul II in the encyclical *Redemptoris Mater* (March 25, 1987):

... the Marian Year is meant to promote a new and more careful reading of what the Council said about the Blessed Virgin Mary, Mother of God, in the mystery of Christ and of the Church, the topic to which the contents of this Encyclical are devoted. Here we speak not only of *the doctrine of faith* but also of *the life of faith,* and thus of authentic "Marian spirituality," seen in the light of Tradition, and especially the spirituality to which the Council exhorts us. Furthermore, Marian *spirituality,* like its corresponding *devotion,* finds a very rich source in the historical experience of individuals and of the various Christian communities present among the different peoples and nations of the world ... (no. 48).

The Church's tradition of honoring the Mother of God has found expression in a number of solemnities and feasts linked to the paschal mystery of Jesus Christ. Likewise, through the centuries, various forms of popular devotion and piety have arisen that have their source both in the liturgy and in Marian spirituality.

Thus, the affirmation of the bishops of the United States of America, in their pastoral letter of 1973 *Behold Your Mother: Woman of Faith,* has taken concrete form:

We Bishops of the United States wish to affirm with all our strength the lucid statements of the Second Vatican Council on the permanent importance of authentic devotion to the Blessed Virgin, not only in the liturgy, where the Church accords her a most special place under Jesus her Son, but also in the beloved devotions that have been repeatedly approved and encouraged by the Church and that are still filled with meaning for Catholics (no. 93).

The celebration of the Marian Year, promulgated by Pope John Paul II, provides a fitting occasion for the publication of these devotions which, it is hoped, will find a suitable place in the prayer life of American Catholics.

Reverend John A. Gurrieri
Executive Director
Secretariat
Bishops' Committee on the Liturgy

Prayers in Honor of the Blessed Virgin Mary

Over the course of centuries, many prayers honoring Mary or addressed directly to her have been written. Many are based on Scripture, such as the "Hail Mary." Others are rooted in ancient devotions or other forms of popular piety. Still others were written by saints who were especially devoted to the Mother of God. This collection by no means exhausts the vast treasury of Marian prayer.

Prayers Addressed to God

Lord our God,
you have made the Virgin Mary
the model for all who welcome your word
and who put it into practice.
Open our hearts to receive it with joy
and by the power of your Spirit
grant that we also may become a dwelling place
in which your Word of salvation is fulfilled.

We ask this through our Lord Jesus Christ, your Son,
who lives and reigns with you and the Holy Spirit,
one God, for ever and ever.

Eternal Father,
you have established in the Virgin Mary

the royal throne of your Wisdom.
Enlighten the Church by the Word of life,
that we may walk in the splendor of truth
and come to full knowledge of your mystery of love.

Grant this through our Lord Jesus Christ, your Son,
who lives and reigns with you and the Holy Spirit,
one God, for ever and ever.

God our Father,
as a root springs forth from fertile soil
so Christ, your Son, by the power of your grace,
was delivered of the Virgin Mary.
Grant that every Christian,
grafted to him through baptism in the Spirit,
may be renewed in youth
and be given the first fruits of grace
   to praise your glory for ever.

We ask this through our Lord Jesus Christ, your Son,
who lives and reigns with you and the Holy Spirit,
one God, for ever and ever.

Holy and merciful God,
you are pleased by the humble
and accomplish in them by means of the Spirit
the great wonders of salvation.
Look upon the innocence of the Virgin Mary,
and give us simple and generous hearts
that respond without hesitation to every sign of
your will.

Grant this through our Lord Jesus Christ, your Son,
who lives and reigns with you and the Holy Spirit,
one God, for ever and ever.

God and Father of the Lord Jesus Christ,
look upon the Virgin Mary,
whose earthly existence was governed
by a spirit of gracious acceptance.
Grant to us also
the gifts of constant prayer and of silence,
that our daily lives may be transfigured
by the presence of your Spirit.

We ask this through our Lord Jesus Christ, your Son,
who lives and reigns with you and the Holy Spirit,
one God, for ever and ever.

Father of holiness,
for the journey of your pilgrim Church on earth,
you have provided the Virgin Mary as a sign and beacon.
Through her intercession
sustain our faith and enliven our hope,
that no obstacle may divert us
from the road which brings us salvation.

Grant this through our Lord Jesus Christ, your Son,
who lives and reigns with you and the Holy Spirit,
one God, for ever and ever.

Gracious God and Father,
in Mary, the first-born of redemption,
you have given us a Mother most tender.
Open our hearts to the joy of the Spirit,
and grant that by imitating the Virgin
we too may learn to magnify you
through the great work accomplished in Christ, your Son.

He lives and reigns with you and the Holy Spirit,
one God, for ever and ever.

Lord our God,
you desired that the Mother of your Son
should be present and joined in prayer
with the first Christian community.
Grant us the grace
to persevere with her in awaiting the Spirit,
that we may be one in heart and mind
and come to taste
the sweet and enduring fruits of redemption.

We ask this through our Lord Jesus Christ, your Son,
who lives and reigns with you and the Holy Spirit,
one God, for ever and ever.

God of eternal glory,
in Christ your Son, sprung from a Virgin Mother,
you have brought true joy to the world.
Free us from the weight of sin
that saddens and extinguishes your Spirit,
and welcome us to the table of your kingdom
where you satisfy us with the bread that contains all
sweetness.

We ask this through our Lord Jesus Christ, your Son,
who lives and reigns with you and the Holy Spirit,
one God, for ever and ever.

God and Father of Christ our Savior,
in Mary, the holy Virgin and attentive Mother,
you have given us the image of your Church.
Send your Spirit to help our weakness,
that we may persevere in faith, grow in love,
and walk together to the heaven of blessed hope.

We ask this through our Lord Jesus Christ, your Son,
who lives and reigns with you and the Holy Spirit,
one God, for ever and ever.

Our Lady of Guadalupe

*In the dioceses of the United States of America, Our
Lady of Guadalupe is celebrated on December 12. The
following is the Opening Prayer of the Mass of the
memorial of Our Lady of Guadalupe.*

God of power and mercy,
you blessed the Americas at Tepeyac
with the presence of the Virgin Mary of Guadalupe.
May her prayers help all men and women
to accept each other as brothers and sisters.

Through your justice present in our hearts
may your peace reign in the world.

We ask this through our Lord Jesus Christ, your Son,
who lives and reigns with you and the Holy Spirit,
one God, for ever and ever.

Amen.

A Prayer from the Maronite Liturgy

The following prayer is taken from "Ramsho" or Evening Prayer (Common of the Blessed Virgin Mary) from the Prayer of the Faithful or Divine Office of the Syriac Maronite Antiochene Church.

Father,
author of all goodness,
we adore you who gave Mary the grace of innocence
   from the time of her conception.
O Son and Word eternal,
we exalt you who appeared in time for our salvation as
   the Son of Mary.
O Holy Spirit, glory be to you who chose Mary as your
   spouse,
for by you all generations proclaim her blessed.
O God,
through her intercession keep us from all harm
and let us always do good by keeping your
   commandments and by pleasing you.
With her we will praise you for ever.
Amen.

Antiphons of the
Blessed Virgin Mary

Alma Redemptoris Mater

*The "Alma Redemptoris Mater," which dates from
the eleventh century, is one of the four antiphons sung
after Night Prayer. It is used in the Advent Season.*

Loving mother of the Redeemer,
gate of heaven, star of the sea,
assist your people who have fallen yet strive to rise
  again.
To the wonderment of nature you bore your Creator,
yet remained a virgin after as before.
You who received Gabriel's joyful greeting,
have pity on us poor sinners.

Alma Redemptoris Mater, quae pervia caeli
porta manes, et stella maris, succurre cadenti,
surgere qui curat, populo: tu quae genuisti,
natura mirante, tuum sanctum Genitorem,
Virgo prius ac posterius, Gabrielis ab ore
summens illud Ave, peccatorum miserere.

Ave Regina Caelorum

The "Ave Regina Caelorum" is one of the four an-tiphons sung after Night Prayer. It is used in Lent.

Hail, Queen of heaven;
Hail, Mistress of the Angels;
Hail, root of Jesse;
Hail, the gate through which the Light rose over the
earth.
Rejoice, Virgin most renowned and of unsurpassed
beauty.

Ave, Regina caelorum,
ave, Domina angelorum,
salve, radix, salve, porta,
ex qua mundo lux est orta.

Gaude, Virgo gloriosa,
super omnes speciosa;
vale, o valde decora,
et pro nobis Christum exora.

Regina Caeli

The "Regina Caeli" is a twelfth-century antiphon for Evening Prayer during the Easter Season. Since the thirteenth century, it has been used as the seasonal antiphon in honor of the Blessed Virgin after Night Prayer.

Queen of heaven, rejoice, alleluia.
The Son whom you merited to bear, alleluia,
has risen as he said, alleluia.
Pray to God for us, alleluia.

Rejoice and be glad, O Virgin Mary, alleluia.
For the Lord has truly risen, alleluia.

Regina caeli, laetare, alleluia:
quia quem meruisti portare, alleluia.
Resurrexit, sicut dixit, alleluia.
Ora pro nobis Deum, alleluia.

Gaude et laetare, Virgo Maria, alleluia.
Quia surrexit Dominus vere, alleluia.

Salve, Regina

The *"Salve, Regina"* is one of the four Marian antiphons sung at the end of Night Prayer, according to the season. It was possibly written by Hermann the Lame, a monk of Reichenau (1013-1054), or by Adhemar, bishop of Le Puy (d. 1098). The *"Salve, Regina"* was also used as a processional antiphon at the Abbey of Cluny (France) from around 1135.

Hail, holy Queen, Mother of mercy,
hail, our life, our sweetness, and our hope.
To you we cry, the children of Eve;
to you we send up our sighs,
mourning and weeping in this land of exile.
Turn, then, most gracious advocate,
your eyes of mercy toward us;
lead us home at last
and show us the blessed fruit of your womb, Jesus:
O clement, O loving, O sweet Virgin Mary.

> Salve, Regina, mater misericordiae;
> vita, dulcedo et spes nostra, salve.
> Ad te clamamus, exsules filii Evae.
> Ad te suspiramus, gementes et flentes
> in hac lacrimarum valle.
>
> Eia ergo, advocata nostra,
> illos tuos misericordes oculos ad nos converte.
> Et Iesum, benedictum fructum ventris tui,
> nobis post hoc exsilium ostende.
> O clemens, o pia, o dulcis Virgo Maria.

Prayers to the Blessed Virgin Mary

The Angelic Salutation

The "Hail Mary" ("Ave Maria") is based on Luke 1:28,42 and is known as the "Angelic Salutation" from the first line of the prayer.

Hail Mary, full of grace,
the Lord is with you!
Blessed are you among women,
and blessed is the fruit of your womb, Jesus.
Holy Mary, Mother of God,
pray for us sinners,
now and at the hour of our death.
Amen.

Ave Maria,
gratia plena, Dominus tecum,
benedicta tu in mulieribus,
et benedictus fructus ventris tui, Iesus.
Sancta Maria, Mater Dei,
ora pro nobis peccatoribus,
nunc et in hora mortis nostrae.
Amen.

Canticle of Mary

The "Canticle of Mary" or "Magnificat" is sung in the celebration of Evening Prayer each day. The text is taken from the Gospel according to Luke 2:29-32.

My soul proclaims the greatness of the Lord,
my spirit rejoices in God my Savior
for he has looked with favor on his lowly servant.
From this day all generations will call me blessed:
the Almighty has done great things for me,
and holy is his Name.

He has mercy on those who fear him
in every generation.

He has shown the strength of his arm,
he has scattered the proud in their conceit.

He has cast down the mighty from their thrones,
and has lifted up the lowly.

He has filled the hungry with good things,
and the rich he has sent away empty.

He has come to the help of his servant Israel
for he remembered his promise of mercy,
the promise he made to our fathers,
to Abraham and his children for ever.

The Angelus

The custom of saying the "Hail Mary" three times at the ringing of the bell in the evening goes back to the thirteenth century. Bells from that period were often inscribed with the the angelic salutation. Today, it is the custom to say the "Angelus" three times: in the morning, at noon, and in the evening. The closing prayer was formerly the postcommunion for Masses of our Lady in Advent and is now the opening prayer for the Fourth Sunday of Advent.

The angel spoke God's message to Mary,
and she conceived of the Holy Spirit.

Hail Mary . . .

"I am the lowly servant of the Lord:
Let it be done to me according to your word."

Hail Mary . . .

And the Word became flesh
and lived among us.

Hail Mary . . .

Pray for us, holy Mother of God,
that we may become worthy of the promises of Christ.

Lord,
fill our hearts with your grace:
once, through the message of an angel
you revealed to us the incarnation of your Son;
now, through his suffering and death
lead us to the glory of his resurrection.
We ask this through Christ our Lord.

Amen.

Regina Caeli

The "Regina Caeli" is a twelfth-century antiphon for Evening Prayer during the Easter Season. Since the thirteenth century, it has been used as the seasonal antiphon in honor of the Blessed Virgin after Night Prayer. From 1743, it has replaced the Angelus in the Easter Season.

Queen of heaven, rejoice, alleluia.
The Son you merited to bear, alleluia,
has risen as he said, alleluia.
Pray to God for us, alleluia.

Rejoice and be glad, O Virgin Mary, alleluia.
For the Lord has truly risen, alleluia.

God of life,
you have given joy to the world
by the resurrection of your Son, our Lord Jesus Christ.
Through the prayers of his mother, the Virgin Mary,
bring us to the happiness of eternal life.
We ask this through Christ our Lord.

Amen.

> Regina caeli, laetare, alleluia:
> quia quem meruisti portare, alleluia.
> Resurrexit, sicut dixit, alleluia.
> Ora pro nobis Deum, alleluia.
>
> Gaude et laetare, Virgo Maria, alleluia.
> Quia surrexit Dominus vere, alleluia.

Sub tuum praesidium
Ancient Prayer to the Virgin

This prayer, known in Latin as "Sub tuum praesidium" and first found in a Greek papyrus, c. 300, is the oldest known prayer to the Virgin.

We turn to you for protection,
holy Mother of God.
Listen to our prayers
and help us in our needs.
Save us from every danger,
glorious and blessed Virgin.

Memorare

The "Memorare" is a sixteenth-century version of a fifteenth-century prayer that began "Ad sanctitatis tuae pedes, dulcissima Virgo Maria." Claude Bernard (1588-1641) popularized the idea that the "Memorare" was written by Saint Bernard.

Remember, most loving Virgin Mary,
never was it heard
that anyone who turned to you for help
was left unaided.

Inspired by this confidence,
though burdened by my sins,
I run to your protection
for you are my mother.

Mother of the Word of God,
do not despise my words of pleading
but be merciful and hear my prayer.

Amen.

Mary, Help of Those in Need

"Mary, Help of Those in Need" was formerly the Magnificat antiphon from the Common of the Blessed Virgin Mary, Evening Prayer.

Holy Mary,
help those in need,
give strength to the weak,
comfort the sorrowful,
pray for God's people,
assist the clergy,
intercede for religious.
May all who seek your help
experience your unfailing protection.

Amen.

A Child's Prayer to Mary

This prayer is from the hymn "Memento rerum conditor." It is also found as the last verse in some versions of the hymn "Quem terra pontus aethera."

Mary, mother whom we bless,
full of grace and tenderness,
defend me from the devil's power
and greet me in my dying hour.

A Prayer for Vocations

This prayer was prepared by the Secretariat of the Bishops' Committee on Vocations, National Conference of Catholic Bishops, in 1987.

Hail Mary, full of grace;
    all generations call you blessed.

Hail Mother of God; when asked by the angel
    to bear the Son of the Most High,
    filled with faith, you responded:
    "Let it be done unto me."

Holy Mother of Jesus, at the wedding feast at Cana,
    you prompted your Son to perform his first sign.

    Be with us as we discern our life's work
    and guide us in the way we are called to follow
    in the footsteps of your Son.

Holy Mother of the Savior, at the foot of the cross
    you mourned the death of your only Son.

    Bless and embrace the loving parents of all priests,
    deacons, brothers, and sisters.

Holy Mother of the Good Shepherd,
    turn your motherly care to this nation.

    Intercede for us to the Lord of the harvest
    to send more laborers to the harvest
    in this land dedicated to your honor.

Queen of Peace, Mirror of Justice, Health of the Sick,
    inspire vocations in our time.

Let the word of your Son be made flesh anew
in the lives of persons anxious to proclaim
the good news of everlasting life.

Amen.

A Hymn of Praise to Mary
from the Byzantine Liturgy

*This hymn of praise known as the "Megalynarion"
(or "Great Hymn to the Theotokos") is taken from the
Divine Liturgy of Saint John Chrysostom of the Byzantine Rite. "Theotokos" (Greek for "God-bearer" or
Mother of God) is Mary's most ancient title.*

It is proper to call you blessed,
ever-esteemed Theotokos, most pure, and mother of
God.
You who are more worthy of honor than the cherubim
and far more glorious than the seraphim.
You who incorruptibly gave birth to God the Word,
verily Theotokos, we fervently extol you.

A Prayer to Mary from the
Act of Entrusting the World to Mary
by Pope John Paul II

Hail to you, Mary,
who are wholly united to the redeeming consecration of
  your Son!

Mother of the Church,
enlighten the people of God along the paths of faith,
  hope, and love.
Help us to live in the truth of the consecration of Christ
for the entire human family of the modern world.

In entrusting to you, O Mother,
the world, all individuals and peoples,
we also entrust to you this very consecration of the
  world,
placing it in your motherly heart.

Immaculate Heart of Mary,
help us to conquer the menace of evil,
which so easily takes root in the hearts of the people
  of today,
and whose immeasurable effects
already weigh down upon our modern world
and seem to block the paths toward the future.

  From famine and war, deliver us.
  From nuclear war, from incalculable self-destruction,
    from every kind of war, deliver us.
  From sins against human life from its very beginning,
    deliver us.
  From hatred and from the demeaning of the dignity
    of the children of God, deliver us.
  From every kind of injustice in the life of society,
    both national and international, deliver us.

From readiness to trample on the commandments of
  God, deliver us.
From attempts to stifle in human hearts the very
  truth of God, deliver us.
From the loss of awareness of good and evil, deliver
  us.
From sins against the Holy Spirit, deliver us.

Accept, O Mother of Christ,
this cry laden with the sufferings of all individual
  human beings,
laden with the sufferings of whole societies.

Help us with the power of the Holy Spirit to conquer
  all sin:
  individual sin and the "sin of the world,"
  sin in all its manifestations.
Let there be revealed once more in the history of the
  world
the infinite saving power of the redemption:
  the power of merciful love.
May it put a stop to evil.
May it transform consciences.
May your immaculate heart reveal for all the light of
  hope.

Amen.

Intercessions

Let us praise God our almighty Father, who wished that Mary, his Son's mother, be celebrated by each generation. Now in need we ask:

You made Mary the mother of mercy,
may all who are faced with trials feel her motherly love.
Mary, full of grace, intercede for us.

You wished Mary to be the mother of the family in the home of Jesus and Joseph,
may all mothers and families foster love and holiness through her intercession.
Mary, full of grace, intercede for us.

You gave Mary strength at the foot of the cross and filled her with joy at the resurrection of your Son,
lighten the hardships of those who are burdened and deepen their sense of hope.
Mary, full of grace, intercede for us.

You made Mary open to your word and faithful as your servant,
through her intercession make us servants and true followers of your Son.
Mary, full of grace, intercede for us.

You crowned Mary queen of heaven,
may all the dead rejoice in your kingdom with the saints for ever.
Mary, full of grace, intercede for us.

"Akathist Hymn"

Hail Mary! Hail, the restoration of the fallen Adam!
    Hail, the redemption of the tears of Eve.
Intercede for us with the Lord.

Hail Mary! Height, hard to climb, for human minds;
    Hail, depth, hard to explore, even for the eyes of
        angels.
Intercede for us with the Lord.

Hail Mary! Throne of wisdom;
    Hail, security and hope for all who call upon you.
Intercede for us with the Lord.

Hail Mary! Heavenly ladder by which God came down
    to earth;
    Hail, bridge leading from earth to heaven.
Intercede for us with the Lord.

Hail Mary! Favor of God to mortals;
    Hail, Mary, access of mortals to God.
Intercede for us with the Lord.

Hail Mary! Mother of the Lamb and of the Good
    Shepherd;
    Hail, fold for the sheep of his pasture.
Intercede for us with the Lord.

Hail Mary! Never silent voice of the apostles;
    Hail, never conquered courage of champions.
Intercede for us with the Lord.

Hail Mary! Mother of the Star which never sets;
    Hail, dawn of the mystic day.
Intercede for us with the Lord.

Hail Mary! Guide of the wisdom of the faithful;
Hail, joy of all generations.
Intercede for us with the Lord.

(Individual petitions are mentioned here.)

Hail Mary! Mother of God's only Son;
Hail, Mother of the Church.
Intercede for us with the Lord.

Litany of the Blessed Virgin Mary

Lord, have mercy	Lord, have mercy
Christ, have mercy	Christ, have mercy
Lord, have mercy	Lord, have mercy
God our Father in heaven	have mercy on us
God the Son, Redeemer of the world	have mercy on us
God the Holy Spirit	have mercy on us
Holy Trinity, one God	have mercy on us
Holy Mary	pray for us
Holy Mother of God	pray for us
Most honored of virgins	pray for us
Chosen daughter of the Father	pray for us
Mother of Christ the King	pray for us
Glory of the Holy Spirit	pray for us
Virgin daughter of Zion	pray for us
Virgin poor and humble	pray for us
Virgin gentle and obedient	pray for us
Handmaid of the Lord	pray for us
Mother of the Lord	pray for us

Helper of the Redeemer	pray for us
Full of grace	pray for us
Fountain of beauty	pray for us
Model of virtue	pray for us
Finest fruit of the redemption	pray for us
Perfect disciple of Christ	pray for us
Untarnished image of the Church	pray for us
Woman transformed	pray for us
Woman clothed with the sun	pray for us
Woman crowned with stars	pray for us
Gentle Lady	pray for us
Gracious Lady	pray for us
Our Lady	pray for us
Joy of Israel	pray for us
Splendor of the Church	pray for us
Pride of the human race	pray for us
Advocate of peace	pray for us
Minister of holiness	pray for us
Champion of God's people	pray for us
Queen of love	pray for us
Queen of mercy	pray for us
Queen of peace	pray for us
Queen of angels	pray for us
Queen of patriarchs and prophets	pray for us
Queen of apostles and martyrs	pray for us
Queen of confessors and virgins	pray for us

Queen of all saints	pray for us
Queen conceived without original sin	pray for us
Queen assumed into heaven	pray for us
Queen of all the earth	pray for us
Queen of heaven	pray for us
Queen of the universe	pray for us
Lamb of God, you take away the sins of the world	spare us, O Lord
Lamb of God, you take away the sins of the world	hear us, O Lord
Lamb of God, you take away the sins of the world	have mercy on us

Pray for us, O glorious Mother of the Lord.
That we may become worthy of the promises of Christ.

God of mercy,
listen to the prayers of your servants
who have honored your handmaid Mary as mother
    and queen.
Grant that by your grace
we may serve you and our neighbor on earth
and be welcomed into your eternal kingdom.

We ask this through Christ our Lord.

Amen.

The Litany of Loreto

The Litany of Loreto, a Marian litany, contains invocations that date back to the twelfth century. It was recorded in its present form (apart from a few additions by recent popes) at Loreto in 1558 and approved by Sixtus V (1521-1590). For about half of the invocations, the present translation uses the traditional renderings, which have been in use since the seventeenth century.

Lord, have mercy	Lord, have mercy
Christ, have mercy	Christ, have mercy
Lord, have mercy	Lord, have mercy
God our Father in heaven	have mercy on us
God the Son, Redeemer of the world	have mercy on us
God the Holy Spirit	have mercy on us
Holy Trinity, one God	have mercy on us
Holy Mary	pray for us
Holy Mother of God	pray for us
Most honored of virgins	pray for us
Mother of Christ	pray for us
Mother of the Church	pray for us
Mother of divine grace	pray for us
Mother most pure	pray for us
Mother of chaste love	pray for us
Mother and virgin	pray for us
Sinless Mother	pray for us
Dearest of mothers	pray for us
Model of motherhood	pray for us
Mother of good counsel	pray for us
Mother of our Creator	pray for us
Mother of our Savior	pray for us
Virgin most wise	pray for us

Virgin rightly praised	pray for us
Virgin rightly renowned	pray for us
Virgin most powerful	pray for us
Virgin gentle in mercy	pray for us
Faithful Virgin	pray for us
Mirror of justice	pray for us
Throne of wisdom	pray for us
Cause of our joy	pray for us
Shrine of the Spirit	pray for us
Glory of Israel	pray for us
Vessel of selfless devotion	pray for us
Mystical Rose	pray for us
Tower of Davis	pray for us
Tower of Ivory	pray for us
House of gold	pray for us
Ark of the covenant	pray for us
Gate of heaven	pray for us
Morning Star	pray for us
Health of the sick	pray for us
Refuge of sinners	pray for us
Comfort of the troubled	pray for us
Help of Christians	pray for us
Queen of angels	pray for us
Queen of patriarchs and prophets	pray for us
Queen of apostles and martyrs	pray for us
Queen of confessors and virgins	pray for us
Queen of all saints	pray for us
Queen conceived without original sin	pray for us
Queen assumed into heaven	pray for us
Queen of families	pray for us
Queen of the rosary	pray for us
Queen of peace	pray for us

Lamb of God, you take away
the sins of the world have mercy on us
Lamb of God, you take away
the sins of the world have mercy on us
Lamb of God, you take away
the sins of the world have mercy on us

Pray for us, holy Mother of God.

That we may become worthy of the promises of Christ.

Let us pray.

Eternal God,
let your people enjoy constant health in mind and body.
Through the intercession of the Virgin Mary
free us from the sorrows of this life
and lead us to happiness in the life to come.

Grant this through Christ our Lord.

Amen.

Prayer to Saint Joseph

While the Fathers of the Church praised Saint Joseph in their writings, devotion to the husband of Mary arose in the Western Church only in the fifteenth century. Pope Leo XIII (1810-1903) encouraged the recitation of this prayer after the rosary and the Litany of Loreto during the month of October.

Blessed Joseph, husband of Mary, be with us this day.

You protected and cherished the Virgin;
loving the Child Jesus as your Son,
you rescued him from danger of death.
Defend the Church, the household of God,
purchased by the blood of Christ.

Guardian of the holy family,
be with us in our trials.
May your prayers obtain for us
the strength to flee from error
and wrestle with the powers of corruption
so that in life we may grow in holiness
and in death rejoice in the crown of victory.

Amen.

Litany of Saint Joseph

The following Litany of Saint Joseph was approved for devotional use by Pope Saint Pius X (1835-1914).

Lord, have mercy	Lord, have mercy
Christ, have mercy	Christ, have mercy
Lord, have mercy	Lord, have mercy
God our Father in heaven	have mercy on us
God the Son, Redeemer of the world	have mercy on us
God the Holy Spirit	have mercy on us
Holy Trinity, one God	have mercy on us
Holy Mary	pray for us
Saint Joseph	pray for us
Noble son of the House of David	pray for us
Light of patriarchs	pray for us
Husband of the Mother of God	pray for us
Guardian of the Virgin	pray for us
Foster father of the Son of God	pray for us
Faithful guardian of Christ	pray for us
Head of the holy family	pray for us
Joseph, chaste and just	pray for us
Joseph, prudent and brave	pray for us
Joseph, obedient and loyal	pray for us

Pattern of patience	pray for us
Lover of poverty	pray for us
Model of workers	pray for us
Example to parents	pray for us
Guardian of virgins	pray for us
Pillar of family life	pray for us
Comfort of the troubled	pray for us
Hope of the sick	pray for us
Patron of the dying	pray for us
Terror of evil spirits	pray for us
Protector of the Church	pray for us

Lamb of God, you take away the sins of the world	have mercy on us
Lamb of God, you take away the sins of the world	have mercy on us
Lamb of God, you take away the sins of the world	have mercy on us

God made him master of his household.
And put him in charge of all that he owned.

Almighty God,
in your infinite wisdom and love
you chose Joseph to be the husband of Mary,
the mother of your Son.
As we enjoy his protection on earth
may we have the help of his prayers in heaven.

We ask this through Christ our Lord.

Amen.

Novena in Honor of the Immaculate Conception of the Blessed Virgin Mary

The custom of praying for nine successive days prior to the celebration of a major solemnity or feast is suggested by the nine days the apostles spent in Jerusalem at the Lord's command as they awaited the coming of the Holy Spirit (see Luke 24:49; Acts 1:4).

The devotional novena first appeared in the Middle Ages in France and Spain as a preparatory period prior to the celebration of Christmas, the number nine (9) representing the nine months Jesus spent in the womb of the Virgin Mary. The "O antiphons" of Advent of the Liturgy of the Hours (December 17-24) are a liturgical vestige of the early Advent novena. Novenas to prepare for the feasts of Mary or one of the saints grew out of that custom. It was not until the nineteenth century that the Church recommended the practice.

The following novena is especially appropriate for the nine days that precede the solemnity of the Immaculate Conception of the Blessed Virgin Mary, December 8. It may be celebrated in public or in private.

Almighty Father,
we offer this novena to honor the Blessed Virgin Mary.
She occupies a place in the Church which is highest
    after Christ
and yet very close to us
for you chose her to give the world
that very Life which renews all things,
Jesus Christ, your Son and our Lord.

And so we praise you, Mary, virgin and mother.
After the Savior himself, you alone are all holy,
free from the stain of sin,
gifted by God from the first instant of your conception
with a unique holiness.

We praise and honor you.

Mary, free from all sin and led by the Holy Spirit,
you embraced God's saving will with a full heart,
and devoted yourself totally as a handmaid of the Lord
to the fulfillment of his will in your life,
and to the mystery of our redemption.

We thank you and love you.

Mary, your privileged and grace-filled origin
is the Father's final step in preparing humanity
to receive its Redeemer in human form.
Your fullness of grace is the Father's sign of his favor to
   the Church
and also his promise to the Church
of its perfection as the Bride of Christ,
radiant in beauty.
Your holiness in the beginning of your life
is the foreshadowing of that all-embracing holiness
with which the Father will surround his people
when his Son comes at the end of time to greet us.

We bless you among all women.

Mary, we turn with confidence to you,
who are always ready to listen with a mother's
   affection
and powerful assistance.
Consoler of the afflicted,

Health of the sick,
Refuge of sinners,
grant us comfort in tribulation,
relief in sickness,
and liberating strength in our weakness.

You who are free from sin, lead us to combat sin.
Obtain for us the victory of hope over anguish,
of joy and beauty over boredom and disgust,
of eternal visions over temporal ones,
of life over death.
Mary, conceived without sin,
pray for us who have recourse to you.

(Individual petitions are mentioned here)

God our Father,
we make these petitions through Mary.
We pray most especially for the coming of your
    kingdom.
May you, together with your Son and the Holy Spirit,
be known, loved and glorified
and your law of love faithfully followed.
We pray in faith through Jesus Christ, your Son and our
    Lord,
in whom all fullness dwells,
now and for ever.

Amen.

Mysteries of the Rosary

The use of the rosary arose in the Middle Ages as a popular form of devotion. Regarded as an offshoot of the liturgy, the rosary has been called "Our Lady's Psalter" because through it the faithful "were enabled to associate themselves with the whole Church's song of praise and intercession" ("Marialis cultus," no. 48). In the rosary, through devout meditation, the mysteries of Christ are called to mind and the faithful are disposed to "celebrate the same mysteries in the rites of the liturgy and then to keep memory of them alive throughout the day" (ibid.).

It is traditional to say all five decades of one of the mysteries of the rosary. According to custom, the joyful mysteries are used on Mondays and Thursdays and on the Sundays of Advent; the sorrowful mysteries are used on Tuesdays and Fridays and on the Sundays of Lent; the glorious mysteries are used on Wednesdays and Saturdays and on the remaining Sundays of the year.

Joyful Mysteries

1. Annunciation of the birth of Jesus to Mary by the angel Gabriel—Luke 1:26-38
2. Visitation of Mary to her cousin Elizabeth—Luke 1:39-47
3. Nativity of our Lord and Savior Jesus Christ—Luke 2:1-7
4. Presentation of the infant Jesus in the Temple—Luke 2:22-32

5.   Finding of the Child Jesus in the Temple by Mary and Joseph—Luke 2:41-52

Sorrowful Mysteries

1.   Agony of Christ in the Garden—Mark 14:32-36
2.   Scourging of Jesus at the Pillar—John 18:28-38; 19:1
3.   Placing of the crown of thorns on the head of Jesus—Mark 15:16-20
4.   Carrying the Cross by Jesus—John 19:12-16
5.   Crucifixion of our Lord Jesus Christ—Luke 23:33-34,39-46

Glorious Mysteries

1.   Resurrection of our Lord from the dead—Luke 24:1-6a
2.   Ascension of our Lord into heaven—Luke 24:50-53
3.   Descent of the Holy Spirit upon the apostles on Pentecost—Acts 2:1-4
4.   Assumption of the Blessed Virgin Mary into heaven—Song of Songs 2:8-14
5.   Coronation of the Virgin Mary—Revelation 12:1-6

Biblical Readings

Contemplating the word of God leads to prayer and meditation.

The following citations from the Old Testament and New Testament refer to readings from The Lectionary for Mass, *"Common of the Blessed Virgin Mary" (nos. 707-712). The citations are provided for use with a Bible. Reading and meditating upon these scriptures will help the individual to understand more deeply Mary's role in the history of salvation.*

Old Testament

Genesis 3:9-15,20—I will put enmity between your offspring and her offspring.

Genesis 12:1-7—He spoke to our fathers, to Abraham and his seed forever.

2 Samuel 7:1-5,8-11,16—God will give him the seat of David his father.

1 Chronicles 15:3-4,15-16; 16:1-2—They brought the ark of God in and put it inside the tent that David had pitched for it.

Proverbs 8:22-31—Mary, seat of wisdom.

Sirach 24:1,3-4,8-12,19-21—Mary, seat of wisdom.

Isaiah 7:10-14—Behold, the virgin shall conceive.

Isaiah 9:1-6—A Son is born to us.

Isaiah 61:9-11—I will rejoice in my God.

Micah 5:1-4—The remnant will return when she who is pregnant gives birth.

Zechariah 2:14-17—Rejoice, daughter of Zion, for I am coming.

New Testament

Matthew 1:1-16,18-23 (Long form)

Matthew 1:18-23 (Short form)—She has conceived and what is in her is by the Holy Spirit.

Matthew 2:13-15,19-23—Take the child and his mother and flee into Egypt.

Luke 1:26-38—You will conceive and bear a Son.

Luke 1:39-47—Blessed is she who believed.

Luke 2:1-14—She gave birth to a Son, her first born.

Luke 2:15-19—Mary treasured all these things and pondered them in her heart.

Luke 2:27-35—A sword will pierce your own soul.

Luke 2:41-52—Your father and I have been looking for you.

Luke 11:27-28—Happy the womb that bore you!

John 2:1-11—The mother of Jesus was at the wedding feast with him.

John 19:25-27—Woman, this is your son. This is your mother.

Acts 1:12-14—They all joined in continuous prayer with Jesus' mother, Mary.

Romans 5:12,17-19—However great the number of sins committed, grace was even greater.

Romans 8:28-30—God knew them and called them to justification.

Galatians 4:4-7—God sent his Son, born of a woman.

Ephesians 1:3-6,11-12—Before the world was made, God chose us in Christ.

Revelation 11:19; 12:1-6,10—A great sign appeared in the heavens.

Revelation 21:1-5—I saw the new Jerusalem, as beautiful as a bride all dressed for her husband.

Psalms and Canticles

1 Samuel 2:1,4-5,6-7,8—My heart rejoices in the Lord, my Savior.

Judith 13:18,19,20—You are the highest honor of our race.

Psalm 45:11-12,14-15,16-17—Listen to me, daughter, see and bend your ear.

Psalm 113:1-2,3-4,5-6,7-8—Blessed be the name of the Lord for ever.

Luke 1:46-47,48-49,50-51,52-53,54-55—The Almighty has done great things for me and holy is his name.